D0374969

maybe
today

maybe today

DAVID BUTLER   EMILY BELLE FREEMAN

ENSIGN
PEAK

Visit us at EnsignPeakPublishing.com

Library of Congress Cataloging-in-Publication Data

Butler, David, author.
  Maybe today : a simple approach to a soul-satisfying life / David Butler, Emily Belle Freeman.
      pages cm
  Includes bibliographical references.
  ISBN 978-1-62972-038-8 (hardbound : alk. paper)
1. Christian life. I. Freeman, Emily, 1969– author. II. Title.
  BV4501.3B9155 2015
  248.4—dc23   2015003587

Printed in China
R. R. Donnelley, Shenzhen, China
10   9   8   7   6   5   4   3   2   1

For Nancy

. . . maybe today

MAYBE TODAY the sun came up just like it always does, And you rolled out of bed just like you always do, And you knew it was going to be one of those days.

JUST ONE OF THOSE DAYS . . .

the kind of day that hints at disappointment, discouragement, and the possibility of failure.

Maybe you are facing tasks that seem beyond your ability to accomplish, or a stack of things left undone.

Perhaps today holds unexpected adventure, filling your heart with the anticipation of good things to come.

Or, maybe today you found yourself weary from waiting on the Lord or in need of courage to face the unknown.

Yes, it's quite possible that this day is one of those.

Your feet hit the floor and you step into the ordinary. You know how it's going to begin:

Start the shower,
plug in to the world,
brush your teeth.

But *maybe today* could be DIFFERENT.

Maybe today you will step out of your routine and step into the soul-satisfying life.

"I went to the woods
because I wished to live
DELIBERATELY,
to front only the essential
facts of life, and see if I could
not learn what it had to teach,
and not, when I came to die,
discover that *I had not lived.*"

—*Henry David Thoreau*

What could you do today to *fill* your soul?

What do you *long* for?

How will you fill your unscheduled *moments?*

This *path* you are on, where is it taking you?

Is your heart *content?*

Could it be that you are missing something?

IF YOU want life to satisfy your soul, you have to start *living* the soul-satisfying life.

It is not an impossible quest.

In fact, there are those who have discovered how.

"Every now and then one meets them, their very VOICES and FACES are different from ours: *stronger, quieter, happier, more radiant.* They begin where most of us leave off. They are, I say, recognizable; but you must know what to look for. . . . They do NOT DRAW ATTENTION to themselves. . . . They LOVE YOU MORE than other men do, but they NEED YOU LESS. They will usually seem to have a lot of TIME; you will wonder where it comes from."

—*C. S. Lewis*

What is it that they KNOW?

Could it be that their days are directed
by *holy patterns?*

It was JESUS who said,
"I am come that they might have
life, and that they might have it
more abundantly."
(John 10:10, KJV)

Jesus wants us to have an
abundant life—to live a
soul-satisfying life.

But that will require us to step out
of the ordinary, to walk His path,
to live His patterns.

MAYBE TODAY

your path could include

five holy patterns.

A simple approach to embracing a

soul-satisfying life.

The 1st Holy Pattern

TILT YOUR SOUL

MAYBE TODAY, as you stumbled into the morning, yesterday's postponed dreams and unaccomplished priorities came rushing back.

They might have come gently, like a *cool summer breeze,* or perhaps they rushed in like a *gale-force wind.*

Head down, you *leaned* into the day.

Where should you go?

What should you DO?

A million things press in on your time, but there's never enough time for a million things.

WHAT IS IT about those first moments that often leaves you feeling scattered?

What if the gentle breeze, the rushing, the gale-force wind could generate power, fill your sail, or cause lift?

Is it possible to channel the rush?

In those first moments it might be worth considering Bernoulli's principle from physics class.

When air is flowing over something—like a plane wing at high speeds—the tilt of the wing becomes crucial.

If the wing is tilted down, it causes
DESCENT.

If the wing is tilted up, it causes LIFT.

Everything depends on the
TILT of the wing.

Such a simple switch can change

the *outcome* so drastically.

So it is with the **TILT OF THE SOUL.**

It matters so much in those first moments.

But how do you tilt the soul?

"Very early in the morning, while
it was still dark, Jesus got up,
left the house and went off to a
solitary place, where he prayed."

(Mark 1:35, NIV)

In those first moments,
JESUS PRAYED.

Where should He go?

What should He do?

The previous evening, just after sunset, "the whole town gathered at the door." (Mark 1:33, NIV)

They had brought their sick, those with pressing needs, pressing in.

It had been a long night.

This morning, the rising of the sun found the crowd gathered again.

Everyone was asking where He was.

So the apostles came looking.

When they found Him, they exclaimed, "Everyone is looking for you." (Mark 1:37, ESV)

"That is why I have come,"
He replied. (Mark 1:38, NIV)

It is why He had sought out a solitary place.

HE KNEW.

Answers come when the day begins with
the soul tilted upward.

That is the pattern of *prayer.*

TILT YOUR SOUL.

PRAYER . . .

directs the rush of the day.

connects you to heaven.

stills and stirs the soul.

answers the questions of the heart.

generates power and causes lift.

When was the last time you received direction through prayer?

"I have been driven many times upon my *knees* by the overwhelming conviction that I had nowhere else to go. My own wisdom and that of all about me seemed *insufficient* for that day."

—*Abraham Lincoln*

PERHAPS you have been driven to your knees. While there, did you think to *pray?*

When your own wisdom seems insufficient, when confusion reigns, when you lack direction, TILT UPWARD.

Solitary moments can be so **soul-satisfying**.

MAYBE TODAY
you will find a *solitary place.*

In those first moments, or the last moments,
or somewhere in the moments in between,
you will live this holy pattern:

TILT YOUR SOUL.

The 2nd Holy Pattern

LET DOWN
YOUR BUCKET

Maybe today *you feel empty.*

Perhaps there are places in your heart that *ache to be filled* or something you long for that the world cannot satisfy.

You try to *fill* the empty places, but it seems you always come up short.

It's not that you don't recognize the inward wants of your soul; it's just that nothing can *quench* your yearning.

On days like today,
    where do you draw STRENGTH?

BOOKER T. WASHINGTON loved to tell a story of the captain of a ship sailing in the South Atlantic. The ship had run out of fresh water, and the entire crew was thirsty.

After several days they sighted a friendly vessel. The captain signaled, "Water, water, we die of thirst!"

The signal came back, *"Let down your bucket where you are."*

A second time the captain signaled, "Water! Send us water!"

Again, the signal came back, *"Let down your bucket where you are!"*

A third and fourth signal for water were returned with the same advice until finally the captain of the friendly ship explained, *"You are in the Amazon. There is fresh water all around you."*

"LET DOWN YOUR BUCKET WHERE YOU ARE."

The crew let down their buckets and immediately realized it was true. They were in the mouth of the mighty Amazon as it flowed into the Atlantic Ocean, and the water all around them was fresh.

The solution to their want had been right there *all along*.

Could the same
be true for YOU?

Could the answer to your want
be CLOSE AT HAND?

COULD YOU LET
DOWN YOUR BUCKET
WHERE YOU ARE?

"SO HE CAME to a town in Samaria. . . . Jacob's Well was there, and Jesus, tired as he was from the journey, sat down by the well. . . . When a Samaritan woman came to draw water Jesus said to her, *will you give me a drink?*" (John 4:5–7, NIV)

The simple question confused her. It was not common for a Jew to associate with a Samaritan. *"How can you ask me for a drink?"* she wondered aloud.

His answer was even more complicated, "If you knew the *gift of God* and *who it is* that asked you for a drink, you would have asked him and he would have given you

living water." (John 4:9–10, NIV)

It was an unexpected meeting at the well.

He, parched from the desert walk.

She, parched from the emptiness of her *soul*.

BOTH ATHIRST.

She with a BUCKET to draw the water.

He, the GIFT OF GOD.

Unanticipated questions led to an unforeseen answer.

> "Everyone who drinks this water
> will be thirsty again,
>
> "But whosoever drinks the water
> I give him will never thirst."
>
> (John 4:13–14, NIV)

In that moment His words changed everything.
The mundane turned to miracle.

It didn't take long for the woman to realize that the
solution to her want had been right there all along.

AT THE WELL.

In ordinary moments,
why shouldn't we expect the

extraordinary?

On that summer afternoon the Lord spoke words that filled the Samaritan woman's empty soul—He spoke to her *heart.*

His words changed her life.

Could His words change YOURS?

Where is the well
that you visit daily?

Is there a quiet place where you can go
to read His words—words that have the power to
change your life?

MAYBE TODAY
you could *set aside time* to commune with the Lord
by turning to sacred verses on *holy pages.*

LET DOWN YOUR BUCKET WHERE YOU ARE.

READING SCRIPTURE...

fills the empty spaces.

provides refuge from the storm.

brings to memory His miracles.

creates companionship and closeness to Him.

enlightens, inspires, guides.

When was the last time your soul was filled through scripture study?

"Occasionally in life there are those *moments* of unutterable fulfillment which cannot be completely explained by those symbols called words. Their meanings can only be articulated by the inaudible *language of the heart.*"

—*Martin Luther King Jr.*

WHEN YOUR HEART is on empty, when the world can't seem to satisfy the inward wants of your soul, when nothing can quench your yearning, *let down your bucket where you are.*

Drinking deeply can be so soul-satisfying— simply sipping won't be enough.

MAYBE TODAY
you will draw from the *words of the Lord.*

In those first moments, or the last moments,
or somewhere in the moments in between,
you will live this holy pattern:

LET DOWN
YOUR BUCKET.

The 3rd Holy Pattern

SEEK A COMPASSIONATE DETOUR

MAYBE TODAY *you wonder*
if you have anything to offer.

Endless demands beg for more and more attention and leave you with less and less to give.

The day fills up before it begins, leaving *no time* for distractions, no space for incidentals, no room for anything that might take you off course.

Here's something that might be worth considering:

Just because your schedule is full doesn't mean your *heart* is.

Days without **purpose** so often lead to a life without **meaning**.

Do you ever lie in bed at night, exhausted, and wonder if you've made a difference?

At the end of the day, you reached your destination, but should you have considered a different route?

Are you ever so set on your own plan that you accidentally miss His?

TWO ROADS diverged in a yellow wood,
And sorry I could not travel both
And be one traveler, long I stood
And looked down one AS FAR as I could
To where it bent in the undergrowth; . . .

I shall be telling this with a sigh
Somewhere ages and ages hence:
Two roads DIVERGED in a wood, and I—
I took the one LESS TRAVELED BY,
And that has made all the DIFFERENCE.

—*Robert Frost*

It doesn't always matter how well you
have planned; every so often your day
comes to a halt unexpectedly.

One path becomes two—
Yours, and HIS.

Sometimes His path will require you
to take a detour.

A detour doesn't mean you won't reach
your *destination;* it just means you
might have to take a *different route.*

Your choice at this fork in the road
makes all the *difference*.

One path is driven by demands,
while MEANING marks the other.

JESUS left the boat and began walking down the dusty path that led into His own city.

Before He could reach His destination, they came to Him, and the day came to a halt unexpectedly before it had even begun. To the paralyzed man lying on the mat, Jesus offered healing. *"Rise, pick up your bed, and go home."* (Matthew 9:6, ESV) He watched the man start walking home, and then returned to His path once more, sandaled feet leaving their mark on the dusty trail.

Before long, He saw Matthew. This time just a short pause, only long enough to extend a simple invitation, *"Follow me."* (Matthew 9:9, KJV)

Lunch was intended to be quiet, but it was interrupted.

First came the publicans and sinners. Then the criticizing Pharisees. Next the questioning disciples of John. Then, again, the day came to a halt unexpectedly when a certain ruler ran into the room, weary and desperate, crying, *"My little daughter is dying, please come and put your hands on her so that she will be healed and live."* (Mark 5:23, NIV)

Without hesitation, Jesus left His lunch and accompanied him, the disciples following close behind.

The route took them down a crowded street. Focused on reaching their destination, they saw only a blur in the faces they passed, until someone touched His robe.

Suddenly one path became two.

Another unexpected halt.

Choosing this path would require
taking a detour—
a compassionate detour.

IT WAS THE MESSAGE
OF HIS LIFE.

The woman was *healed*.
The daughter was *raised from the dead*.
The blind received their *sight*.
He who was mute *spoke*.

"And Jesus went about all the cities and villages, teaching in their synagogues, and preaching the gospel of the kingdom, and healing every sickness and every disease among the people.

"But when He saw the multitudes, he was MOVED WITH COMPASSION on them. . . ."
(Matthew 9:35–36, KJV)

JESUS WAS MOVED WITH COMPASSION.

When life came to a halt unexpectedly,
He took the detour.

He lived on purpose,
and life became *meaningful.*

SEEK A
COMPASSIONATE
DETOUR.

SERVICE...

expands your capacity to love.

creates a heart like His.

magnifies your gifting.

allows you to be the difference.

When was the last time you were
moved with compassion?

"Not all
of us can do
great things…
but we can do
small things
with great
LOVE."

—*Mother Teresa*

Today, *if one path becomes two,*

CHOOSE HIS.

When you wonder if you have *anything to offer,* when life comes to an unexpected halt, when you long to make a *difference,*

SEEK A COMPASSIONATE DETOUR.

Moving with compassion can be so soul-satisfying.

MAYBE TODAY
you will walk a path marked with *meaning.*

In those first moments, or the last moments,
or somewhere in the moments in between,
you will live this holy pattern:

SEEK A
COMPASSIONATE
DETOUR.

The 4th Holy Pattern

TAKE OFF
YOUR SHOES

Maybe today
you wish things could be different.

It's not that the sky is falling, but it isn't necessarily blue, either. *It's partly cloudy with a chance for rain.* Things are just *okay.* In general, life is *good enough,* but some days you struggle to find enough good.

No matter how much you try, you can't seem to shake the fact that today feels a half size too small.

There's only one remedy
for a day like this:

Don't just pick the
BLACKBERRIES.

Earth's crammed with *heaven,*

And every common bush
afire with God,

But only he who *sees*
takes off his shoes;

The rest sit round it and
pluck *blackberries.*

—*Elizabeth Barrett Browning*

IN THE MOMENTS when life is crammed full of common things and your heart begins to fill with discontent, you might need to look for a *burning bush*.

Every day is filled with blessings from the Lord. They are all around—*surrounding us*.

Somehow we see, and yet we do not SEE.

How long has it been since your heart filled with gratitude for the mercies that fill your life?

WHEN WAS THE LAST TIME YOU TOOK OFF YOUR SHOES?

"Now Moses was tending the flock of Jethro, his father in law. . . . And he led the flock to the far side of the wilderness" and came to the mountain of God. (Exodus 3:1, NIV)

Just a flock of sheep, a wilderness, and a bush on the mountainside—everything so common *until the bush burned with fire.*

Moses looked.
He noticed.
He turned aside to see.

When the Lord saw that Moses turned aside to see,
He called to him and said, "Take your sandals off
your feet, for the place on which you are
standing is *holy ground.*" (Exodus 3:5, ESV)

WHY DID MOSES TAKE OFF HIS SANDALS?

Perhaps it was out of duty—maybe he was
simply following a commandment from the Lord.

Or could it have been out of
recognition for God's mercy,
out of awe,
out of gratitude?

Perhaps Moses's life wasn't exactly where he wanted it to be.

Maybe things were just okay.

Then a common bush caught fire with God, and the wilderness filled with *heaven,* and Moses took off his shoes. He took off his shoes because *he turned aside* and saw heaven in the wilderness.

He took off his shoes in recognition, in awe,

in gratitude.

He took off his shoes because common terrain suddenly became *holy ground*.

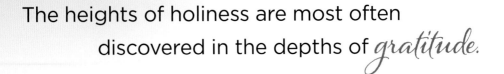

The heights of holiness are most often discovered in the depths of *gratitude*.

TAKE OFF
YOUR SHOES.

GRATITUDE...

views the world the way God intends it to be seen.

brings to light what truly surrounds us.

looks past what we lack.

discovers the good.

When was the last time you viewed your life
through the lens of gratitude?

"O Thou who has

given us so much,

mercifully grant us

one thing more,

a *grateful heart."*

—George Herbert

When you wish things were different,
when you are feeling discontent,
when you can't find enough good . . .

TAKE OFF YOUR SHOES.

A *grateful heart* can be so
soul-satisfying.

MAYBE TODAY
you will turn aside *to see.*

In those first moments, or the last moments,
or somewhere in the moments in between,
you will live this holy pattern:

TAKE OFF
YOUR SHOES.

The 5th Holy Pattern

BE ALL
IN

MAYBE TODAY you just want to
choose the path of *least resistance.*

Perhaps you feel like you've been trying a
little *too hard* for a little *too long.*

Think back:
Can you remember the last time
passion led to motivation?

When you live your life just going through the
motions, what used to be *exhilarating*
becomes just plain exhausting.

A TRAVELER stood at the desk of a European hotel admiring the photo on the wall—a man hang-gliding against a magnificent mountain backdrop.

"Are those the Alps?" she asked the man standing behind the desk.

"Yes," he replied with a grin, "and that's me. Would you like me to take you?"

Momentarily thrilled, and completely against her *natural inhibitions,* she immediately agreed.

The next day at breakfast, he approached her. "The weather is perfect. Maybe today would be a good day."

The gondola ride ended in the middle of a lush, green meadow.

He knelt down to prepare the glider, and she took in the scenery. It was *picturesque.* Cows wandered the meadow, their copper bells gently clanging as they walked. Billowy, white clouds dotted the deep blue sky. A flock of sheep surrounded the clearing.

The world stood still.

Before long all was ready. The man with the scruffy beard, blond hair, and ice-blue eyes stood and began clearing the sheep out of the way.

There would have to be room to RUN.

He directed her attention to a pole hammered into the ground beside the cliff with a tattered red ribbon tied to the top.

Then, in a thick European accent, he began giving her the list of instructions: "I'll watch the ribbon for the wind to pick up. When I say GO, we will start running toward the cliff.

"You must *not stop* running under any circumstance. You will *want* to. But you *must not stop.* Once we start running, you have to BE ALL IN."

It was at that moment the *hesitation* filled her heart.

But before she could say anything, the wind lifted the tattered ribbon, and the man yelled, "GO!"

Together, they ran toward the edge of the cliff, grasping the rod of the glider. *Against all reason,* they picked up speed as they neared the edge.

In that split second, as she watched the edge of the earth drop off below her, she took a step into the *unknown,* she felt the rush of the wind lift the kite, and they FLEW.

In moments of *greatest consequence,*
it's not the thought of *sacrifice* that
holds us back, it's the fear of what
the sacrifice will REQUIRE.

LIFE ALTERS when we choose to let *yes* be our first response. Moments become defining when our decisions are governed by courage. Change happens when we step into the unknown.

Sometimes the soul-satisfying life
requires us to do hard things.

He was a man small of stature, important but often overlooked. Life was all about the numbers, the routine, the familiar. Nothing more meant nothing less. Every day it was the same.

He walked the street that day completely caught up in the numbers, and then he saw the crowd. He knew what they were waiting for, watching for. For a split second he paused, wanting to know who *He* was, the man they were so anxious to see.

Zacchaeus couldn't see over the pressing crowd.
After glancing around, he quickly realized there
was only one option available:

A SYCAMORE TREE.

DO GROWN MEN CLIMB TREES?
Educated men? Important men?

It was a question he must have considered.

Little did he know that this decision
was about to *alter* his life.

Zacchaeus dug inside himself, found courage waiting there, and approached the tree.

The branches with their green leaves were unfamiliar territory for a tax collector.

It was the first of many changes the Lord held in store for him that day.

He grabbed hold of the lowest branch and began to climb. There was no turning back now— Zacchaeus had made up his mind, and once committed, he was ALL IN.

It wasn't long before *He* came walking down the street: JESUS, the man who had occupied the conversation of the town for days. Zacchaeus watched Him move through the crowd, weaving through the people, and then *He* stopped.
Right under Zacchaeus's tree.

"Zacchaeus," he said, "make haste and come down, for today I must stay at your house." (Luke 19:5, ESV)

Out of all the people in the crowd, Jesus had chosen ONE.

A man small of stature, important
but often overlooked.

A man whose life was about to be
altered, changed, defined.

Because he climbed a tree.

He did something out of the
ordinary, something that
required his *heart, might,
mind, and strength,*
in an attempt to know
more of the LORD.

ZACCHAEUS knew what it meant to step into the unknown. To leave his comfort zone. *To stretch.*

This man, who gave half of his goods to the poor, who restored fourfold to those who falsely accused him, had come to understand an *important life lesson* that is so often overlooked:

If you want to experience a soul-satisfying life, *it will require commitment, sacrifice, and heart.*

BE ALL IN.

COMMITMENT . . .

takes sacrifice and courage.

is born of determination, dedication, and desire.

requires us to do hard things.

understands that achieving impossibilities
 sometimes requires letting go of possibilities
 that have become too familiar.

deepens character, stretches capacity,
 and overcomes apathy.

What tree do you intend
to climb today?

"HANG ON THE WALLS OF YOUR MIND

the memory of your *successes.* Take counsel

of your *strength,* not your weakness. Think

of the good jobs you have done. Think of the

times when you *rose above* your average level

of performance and carried out an idea or a

dream or a desire for which you had deeply

longed. Hang these pictures on the walls of

your mind and look at them as you

travel the roadway of life."

—James McNeill Whistler

ARE YOU READY to leave your comfort zone?

Is your life giving you the
opportunity to SOAR?

WHEN YOU ARE TEMPTED to choose the path of least resistance, when you lack motivation, when you are living life just going through the motions,

BE ALL IN.

Defining moments can be so soul-satisfying.

MAYBE TODAY
you will commit to something
that will *stretch you.*

In those first moments, or the last moments,
or somewhere in the moments in between,
you will live this holy pattern:

BE ALL IN.

MAYBE TODAY the sun came up just like it always does, And you rolled out of bed just like you always do, And you knew it was going to be one of those days.

BUT MAYBE TODAY WILL BE DIFFERENT.

MAYBE TODAY you will begin to realize it's not about you—*it's about Him.*

The One who never lived an *ordinary day.*

The One who leads to the soul-satisfying life.

IT'S ABOUT JESUS.

Every minute. Every hour. Every day.

Could He become the *pattern* of your life?

WHEN YOU LACK DIRECTION,
when you can't seem to fill the empty spaces,
when you wonder if you have anything to offer,
when things are just okay,
when going through the motions is just
plain exhausting,

STEP OUT OF THE
ORDINARY.

*A life with Jesus can be so
soul-satisfying.*

Maybe today
you will let Him *satisfy your soul.*

In those first moments, or the last moments,
or somewhere in the moments in between,
you will live His holy patterns:

TILT YOUR SOUL

LET DOWN YOUR BUCKET

SEEK A
COMPASSIONATE DETOUR

TAKE OFF YOUR SHOES

BE ALL IN

He knows your *heart.*

Live your life so you
can come to know

HIS.

Because one day He is going to

COME AGAIN.

MAYBE TODAY.

multiply
GOODNESS

This book is meant to be shared.
We want you to give it away.
As you turned each page, did someone come to mind?
Someone you love.
Someone in need.
Could this message bring good into their life?
Then pass it along, and multiply goodness.

The world needs more good!
For more ways to share it,
visit *www.multiplygoodness.com*

IMAGE CREDITS

About the Authors

DAVID BUTLER is by day a high school religious educator sharing his love for the scriptures and his belief that there is a power for good innate in every human soul. By night he is a fort builder, waffle maker, sports coach, and storyteller for his six favorite little people, also known as his children. Somewhere in between he is a motivational speaker and writer. He is the coauthor of the blog www.multiplygoodness.com. He and his wife, Jenny, live with their family amid the snowcapped peaks of the Mountain West, but they often dream of a beach house on a sunny shore somewhere.

EMILY BELLE FREEMAN is a coach's wife, mother to five children and a few others who have found refuge in her home, author of several bestselling books, and sought-after inspirational speaker. Her days are spent watching over teenagers, her flock of pampered chickens, and a rabbit that she adores. She finds great joy in studying the life and teachings of Jesus Christ. Her deep love of the scriptures comes from a desire to find their application in everyday life. For a few minutes every day Emily forgets about the laundry, leaves the dishes in the sink, and writes. She coauthors a blog that is a stopping place for hearts seeking all that is good: www.multiplygoodness.com.